CRYPTOCURRENCY INCOME TAX PLANNING

A Tax Brief

Robert L. Sommers

Sommers-Taxapedia.com

Second Edition

ISBN-10: 0-9778616-2-7
ISBN-13: 978-0-9778616-2-0

Cover art and layout by Crawshaw Design

Sommers-Taxapedia.com

Printed in the United States of America

About the Author

Robert L. Sommers provides sophisticated legal advice concerning complex tax, business and estate planning issues.

As an acknowledged expert in the field of tax law, Bob has written hundreds of articles, columns, and action guides and spoken at dozens of events.

Bob Sommers is The Tax Prophet. He has created and written The Tax Prophet website, a vital resource to those seeking solid U.S. tax information, issue spotting and analysis.

As a full-time practicing attorney in the heart of San Francisco's Financial District, Bob owns and operates a general tax law firm.

He focuses on U.S. and foreign individuals and small companies in the areas of

- Estate planning (wills, trusts and family-based entities)
- Foreign tax
- Business start-ups and funding
- Employee stock options
- Probate and trust administration
- Federal and California tax controversies (audits, appeals and litigation)

Certified as a Tax Specialist by the California Board of Legal Specialization of the State Bar of California (a distinction earned by less than .05% of all attorneys licensed to practice law in California,) Bob also received a postgraduate legal degree (LL.M.) in taxation from New York University School of Law in 1985, the premier graduate tax program in the U.S.

Bob has testified before the US Senate's Finance Committee regarding tax scams on the Internet. He is in demand as an expert witness in both criminal and civil cases involving Tax and Trust Law, Tax Fraud, Busted Tax Shelters, and Bogus Trust Arrangements.

The Wall Street Journal, New York Times, Forbes, CNN to Money magazine and the Best of the Web have all reviewed Bob's work and his contributions to legal education. Reviews online.

CONTENTS

I. Preliminary Matters..1

II. Income Tax Issues...3

III. Recordkeeping and Reporting Requirements...................10

IV. Creative Income Tax Planning...16

V. Conclusion 28

Exhibit "A" 29

Exhibit "B" 30

Exhibit "C" 37

Exhibit "D" 41

CRYPTOCURRENCY INCOME TAX PLANNING

Disclaimer: This Tax Brief is written for the general public concerning federal income tax issues and planning techniques. The author is fully aware that each situation is unique and there are many caveats, limitations and restrictions throughout the tax law that must be considered when implementing an actual tax strategy. This Tax Brief provides a general discussion of the primary issues only and does not constitute tax advice or recommendations. Always consult with a knowledgeable and experienced tax advisor licensed in your jurisdiction before engaging in any tax-related transaction.

I. Preliminary Matters

A. Introduction

This Tax Brief focuses on U.S. federal income tax consequences of investing in cryptocurrencies on a regular or long-term basis. It is not intended for cryptocurrency miners or those holding cryptocurrencies for sale to customers. There are on-line sources describing how to calculate your gains and losses from cryptocurrency trades, but there is a lack of guidance on planning cryptocurrency investments to minimize taxes. This Tax Brief is written from the perspective of an experienced tax attorney and discusses successful tax-planning techniques he has developed through decades of research and experience.

B. Defining Cryptocurrency

Cryptocurrencies have been defined in a variety of ways. Basically, for this Tax Brief cryptocurrency is defined as internet money, the currency of the internet and supported by the internet's confidence in that money. Technically, it is a method of payment without physical form and exists on public blockchain ledgers (such as Bitcoin or Ethereum). Unlike electronic bank payments or transactions, cryptocurrencies are not linked to actual currencies. The price is usually represented in U.S. dollars or Euros.

In contrast, physical money ("fiat currency") is backed by the government of that country and must be accepted as legal tender – it is the confidence in that country's ability to maintain the value of its currency that determines the price. For example, a country with rampant inflation will have low or no confidence in its currency and, most likely, a black market in dollars or Euros will emerge. In fact, some countries, including El Salvador, Equator and Zimbabwe have abandoned their currencies in favor of U.S. dollars. Cryptocurrencies function in generally the same manner – as a virtual convertible currency financed by internet users rather than countries.

C. IRS Definition of Cryptocurrency

IRS treats cryptocurrency not as equivalent to paper money, but as intangible personal property,[1] somewhat akin to stock or securities. Each time there is a transaction involving cryptocurrency, taxable gain or loss occurs. This creates a potential record-keeping nightmare for buyers and sellers of cryptocurrencies since wherever a currency is sold, traded or exchanged, a taxable event occurs. In contrast, if cryptocurrencies were considered cash instead of property, trading between one cryptocurrency and another (much like exchanging U.S. dollars for Euros) would not cause taxable income.

---

1 Intangible property is property that does not exist in physical form and has no intrinsic value. For example, a stock certificate has no intrinsic value -- it's a piece of paper -- but it represents value, a number of shares at a certain price. Examples of intangibles include securities, intellectual property, patents and copyrights.

II. Income Tax Issues

A. Basic Taxation of Cryptocurrency

Because cryptocurrencies are considered property, their sale, trade or exchange creates capital gains or losses. If the currency is held for less than one year, the gain or loss is short-term (taxed at ordinary income rates). Conversely, if the currency is held for 12 months or longer, the gain or loss will be long-term and there are favorable federal tax rates for long-term capital gains (capital gain rates are attached as Exhibit "A").

> For example, if you buy pizza worth $20.00 with cryptocurrency you acquired for $2.00, you have a capital gain of $18.00 and the pizza seller has $20.00 of ordinary income and the seller has a new basis in the currency of $20.00. If seller later sells, exchanges or transfers the currency for $12.00, seller now has a $8.00 capital loss, but guess what, the capital loss does not offset the $20.00 of business income since each is treated differently – as two separate transactions. This simple example of using cryptocurrency for payment of goods or services illustrates the potential for tax entanglements.

In reality, cryptocurrencies function both as property and currency. Thus far, IRS has characterized cryptocurrencies as intangible personal property subject to the same rules as purchase, trades, exchanges or sales of stock, i.e. either short-term or long-term capital gains or losses. See IRS Notice 2014-21 and the update thereto dated

October 8, 2019, as frequently asked questions (attached hereto as Exhibit "B").

B. No Like-Kind Exchanges after 2017

Because cryptocurrencies are considered property, the tax-free like-kind exchange rules of Internal Revenue Section 1031 should apply when one coin is exchanged for another since they are like-kind. Under Section 1031, in general, an exchange of property held for investment for property of a like-kind held for investment defers taxes on the property received until there is an actual sale. Real estate investors use Section 1031 to trade-up their real estate investments without taxation.

Congress clarified that commencing in 2017, Section 1031 could not be utilized for exchanges of cryptocurrencies. Prior to 2017, the like-kind exchange provisions should apply, since if cryptocurrencies were never covered by Section 1031 in the first place, Congress would not have removed them from Section 1031 after tax year 2016.

C. Receipt of a Hard Fork Coin

A hard fork involves receipt of additional cryptocurrency, usually a new form of an existing blockchain, such as Bitcoin Cash or Ethereum Classic. A hard fork coin can be created by anyone, so unless a market develops in the new coin, it has no value. Also, exchanges will not accept a hard fork unless the exchange concludes the coins have legitimate value; thus, merely creating a hard fork without buy-in from the cryptocurrency community should be a non-event for tax purposes.

IRS has not provided guidance regarding the receipt of a hard fork. Absent IRS input, the most sensible approach is to treat its receipt as a taxable event once the cryptocurrency community accepts or supports it (which could occur instantly or never) and the owner has the unrestricted right to own it (including the right to sell it). The value of the hard fork is the fair market value on date of receipt, if the value can be ascertained, or treated as zero value (the basis in the hard fork is zero) on the date of acquisition if there is not a market for the coin, there have been no trades and there is not another method to value it. Under this approach, the investor has a zero-cost basis in the coin and upon sale, the entire gain is taxable. Sometimes, hard fork coins are received by investors without request or notice, so ownership of the new coin should not occur until the investor possesses it. This requires that the investor know or should have known about the hard fork coin; likewise, an immediately rejection should remove potential tax concerns.

CRYPTOCURRENCY INCOME TAX PLANNING

> Example: A hard fork for Cryptocurrency A created, coin B. Taxation of coin B should occur only when the cryptocurrency community accept coin B as having value, and the owner of A knows (or should have known) about coin B, has the right to possess it, including the right to sell it, and does not immediately reject it. At the time of ownership, coin B is valued at its fair market value if one can be established; otherwise it should be valued at zero. Ownership commences the holding period for capital gains. If coin B has no value when ownership occurs, a later sale will be fully taxable; if coin B is held for 12 months or longer, long-term capital gains rates apply.

Note: After the initial publication of this Tax Brief, IRS essentially confirmed the tax treatment of a hard fork as described herein. See Revenue Ruling 2019-24 dated October 9, 2019) attached hereto as Exhibit "C".

One way to establish the value of a hard fork is to immediately sell it upon receipt. If there is not market or it cannot be sold, then the value would be zero. If you received $1.00 per new coin, then the FMV would be $1.00. Selling and repurchasing the same new coin will establish the value for tax purposes and leave the owner in the same economic position. Of course, if you sell the currency for a substantial amount, it would be prudent to withhold the tax amount on the sale and repurchase the sold item with the balance of the proceeds, just in case the new currency crashes in value.

CRYPTOCURRENCY INCOME TAX PLANNING

D. Two Major Tax Traps

1. Profits in Year One, Losses in Year Two

Beware: Trading in cryptocurrencies carries a huge tax risk! Losses from one calendar year cannot be carried back to offset gains from prior years. This drawback often occurs with day traders of securities and others who do not understand how the capital gain and loss rules work. Consequently, taxpayers can generate a huge tax without retaining sufficient assets to pay it.

> Example: Assume in year one taxpayer has a gain of $5.0 million from the sale or exchange of cryptocurrencies held less than one year. In tax year 2, he has a loss of $4.0 million. Common sense would dictate that the loss of $4.0 million should offset the gain of $5.0 million since, after all, the taxpayer only has $1.0 million of wealth that should be subject to tax.

Wrong answer! The $5.0 million is fully taxable, but the subsequent loss cannot be carried back to offset the loss. The loss may be used against ordinary income at the rate of $3,000 a year moving forward and may offset any future capital gains, but our taxpayer is stuck with a tax of potentially $2.0 million with only $1.0 million left to pay it! Unfortunately, this has occurred to some cryptocurrency investors because of wild swings in values, causing large gains and losses to quickly emerge.

2. Cryptocurrency as Payment for Goods and Services

Receiving cryptocurrency as payment creates ordinary business income, but the asset itself is subject to capital gains and losses, so the cryptocurrency recipient has ordinary income as to the fair market value of the product being sold or service performed, whether or not the cryptocurrency thereafter increases or decreases in value. It is as though the item were sold for shares of corporate stock; the transaction itself produces ordinary income, but the stock is an investment asset in the hands of the recipient. The same pitfall may if a vendor sold a large portion of inventory or services in exchange for cryptocurrency and it later dropped in value. The vendor cannot offset business income with cryptocurrency losses.

3. Summary – Avoid the Lurking Tax Traps

Be cognizant of your gain or loss position and make sure you sell loss positions by the end of the calendar year to offset gains during the year. Selling the loss positions in the subsequent year can lead to disaster, because you cannot carry them back. For merchants and service providers, make sure your cryptocurrency transactions comprise a fraction of your business transactions or sell them immediately to protect yourself against a devaluation; remember, your income is based on the price of the product or service sold and not the subsequent value of the cryptocurrency.

E. Harvest Losses at the End of the Year

Taxpayers with cryptocurrency losses can sell those positions, recognize the loss then immediately repurchase the position, without running afoul of the wash sales rules under Internal Revenue Code Section 1091. The wash sales rule is limited to sales and repurchases of securities, not cryptocurrencies. In general, a loss is not counted if the same or substantially identical stock is repurchased within 30 days of the sale.

> Example, Joe owns 100 shares of IBM stock that has a loss of $100,000. On December 1st, he buys 100 shares at the depressed valuation, then on December 29th, he sells his 100 of loss shares. Section 1091 does not allow the recognition of the loss since Joe purchased identical shares within 30 days of triggering the loss. The same result will occur if Joe sold the loss shares on December 29th then repurchased the same stock on January 25th.

Because the wash sales rule does not apply, cryptocurrencies may be sold for a loss and then repurchased immediately. This is a significant tax break that should be utilized at the end of each calendar year.

III. Recordkeeping and Reporting Requirements

A. Recordkeeping

Because IRS treats cryptocurrencies as property, for each purchase you'll need to keep copious records of the date purchased, quantity, price and total amount paid. For each sale, you'll need to know the date sold, quantity and price. You'll need the same information each time you trade or exchange one for another or use it for purchases products or services. Likewise, if you accept cryptocurrencies as payment, you will need to record the date received, quantity, price and total amount.

Cryptocurrency exchanges may maintain some or all of this information, but to protect yourself against a sudden exchange shutdown, you need to separately maintain these records, preferably in accounting software designed for this task (Quicken, QuickBooks, or another financial/investment tracking software), or if need be, in an Excel spreadsheet. Note: CPAs and tax preparers often look askance at records maintained in Excel spreadsheets since the traditional accounting functions and protections are missing.

B. Identification of Cryptocurrencies That Are Sold

In general, IRS insists on the first-in, first-out method of accounting (FIFO) when a specific asset is difficult to identify, including cryptocurrencies. Unless you can specifically identity your asset, perhaps it is held in a separate account or wallet, use FIFO to account for your sales.

> For example, say you purchased Bitcoin on different dates over a 24-month period. When you sell Bitcoin, FIFO states that you are selling the oldest purchase first, which could generate the largest gain if you paid a low price. Also, it may tax the gain at favorable long-term capital gain rates. This can be a major problem if you want to hold on to your old Bitcoin purchases and sell your recent acquisitions.

Unless you can adequately identify your purchases – by using separate wallets for each acquisition and not co-mingling two or more purchases within a single wallet, thereby allowing you to identify the asset being sold – you need to use FIFO.

C. Don't Trust Your Exchange to Retain Critical Information

I've heard horror stories about cryptocurrency exchanges disappearing or being shutdown and none of the taxpayers' trading records are retrievable. Also, watch out for foreign currency exchanges. Sometimes, your domestic bank will not accept transfers from a foreign cryptocurrency exchange (the concern is money laundering or illegal activities) so you could wind up owing U.S. taxes on your cryptocurrency income, have the money sitting in a foreign exchange, but are unable to retrieve the funds to pay your taxes! In addition, depending on the activities of the foreign exchange, you could have a foreign bank report, an FBAR and a Form 8938 filing requirement (discussed later).

D. Domestic Exchanges and Reporting Requirements

A U.S.-based cryptocurrency exchange must comply with IRS requests for information and should report trading activities on Form 1099-K when they exceed $20,000 or 200 transactions per year. This form reports the total amount of your trades and does not calculate gains or losses. You are obligated to file a tax return to report your actual gains or losses. If IRS receives a Form 1099-K and you do not file a tax return, IRS will treat the entire amount as taxable and send you a bill based on this amount. Your remedy is to file an accurate tax return. Note: If you are a vendor or service provider, cryptocurrency payments may generate a Form 1099 reporting obligations.

E. Foreign Reporting Requirements

If you hold cryptocurrencies on a foreign exchange, IRS could classify the exchange as a bank, thus triggering foreign reporting requirements. In general, if your cryptocurrencies can be converted into currency and transmitted to another financial institution, if the account earns interest, if you can withdraw funds from the account with an ATM or use a debit card for purchases with cryptocurrency or cash, the account will be subject to foreign reporting requirements. Merely holding cryptocurrencies on a foreign exchange with no possibility of the exchange transmitting funds to another bank or providing the other described services should not trigger the FBAR and Form 8938 foreign reporting requirements,[2] but stay tuned since this is an evolving area of the law.

1. FBARS (Report of Foreign Bank and Financial Accounts)

If your foreign exchange meets the tests for a foreign financial institution, then invariably, you must file annual FBARS, reporting the highest balance in the account during the year. The FBAR is a foreign financial account reporting duty, it is not involved with taxation. In general, anyone with ownership or signature authority (co-owner, power of attorney, fiduciary) over one or more foreign financial accounts (in general, banks, brokerage accounts, life insurance with a cash value or other accounts in which assets may be converted into cash) that, in total, meet or exceed $10,000 during any time within a calendar year, must report all the accounts on an FBAR. The due date is the due date of your tax return, with regard to

2 See U.S. v Hom, No. 14-16214 (2016), an unpublished 9th Circuit Court opinion stating that an on-line gambling website that did not transmit funds to another bank was not a foreign financial account for FBAR purposes.

extensions. The penalty for non-willful failure to file an FBAR can be as high as $10,000 per year, per account, for six years. Taxpayers complete the FBAR on-line and the form is relatively simple once you determine the highest amount in each of your accounts during the year. The penalty may be eliminated upon an affirmative showing of reasonable cause and there are various IRS amnesty-type programs that reduce or eliminate the penalty.

2. Form 8938

In addition to FBARs, starting in 2011 taxpayers with foreign financial account and certain other financial assets, generally, bank and brokerage accounts, individually held stock, securities or interests in foreign entities (including family owned entities), and certain employee stock benefit plans must report those assets on Form 8938, which is filed with the Form 1040. If your foreign exchange has the attributes of a foreign financial institution described above, then you could have a Form 8938 obligation.

There are minimum thresholds that apply, depending on whether taxpayers are single or joint filers and whether they live in the U.S. The penalty for failure to file Form 8938 is $10,000 per delinquent filing and there is no statute of limitations until the form is filed. The penalty may be eliminated upon an affirmative showing of reasonable cause and there are various IRS amnesty- type programs that reduce or eliminate the penalty.

IV. Creative Income Tax Planning

A. The Economic Substance Doctrine

The U.S. Supreme Court has consistently affirmed that taxpayers may engage in tax planning to lower their taxes to the legal minimum; there is no duty to pay the government more. However, the Supreme Court has also stated that the tax law operates on real deals with economic substance and tax planning devoid of economic substance will be ignored. Therefore, when considering various tax-planning strategies, bear in mind that each transaction should be tested for economic substance and cannot just be a paper transfer. In short, this planning should not be undertaken without the assistance of an experienced tax professional who understands the economic substance doctrine and how it could apply to your particular situation.

Note: There is not an economic substance concern if Congress expressly authorized the transaction in the tax code. For instance, the following transactions described below: forming a C corporation; donations to charity; using charitable trusts; funding retirement plans; and using Qualified Opportunity Zones are sanctioned in the tax code. The challenge with these transactions is ensuring compliance with existing tax law.

CRYPTOCURRENCY INCOME TAX PLANNING

B. Use a C Corporation

A C corporation is a separate taxpaying entity. Prior to 2017, C corporations were taxed at a maximum federal rate of 35%; the 2017 tax act lowered the corporate tax to 21%. This compares favorably to the highest federal individual tax rate of 38.8%. However, if a C corporation makes dividend distributions to individual taxpayers, the dividends are taxed at capital gains rates, so there is a potential double tax on corporate income, once at the C corporation level and again at the shareholder level. If the goal is to invest and reinvest in cryptocurrencies (or any other investment asset, such as stock or securities) for the long term, the initial savings in taxes by using a C corporation should outstrip the potential for a shareholder-level tax down the road. The earnings of the corporation may be used to fund family real estate ventures or other investments, without triggering a tax on dividends. Think of the C corporation as a family bank in this regard. If income is needed, reasonable salaries may be paid; the recipient will pay ordinary income on the compensation and the corporation will deduct the payments. **Note:** This transaction is relatively straight forward and should not run afoul of the economic substance doctrine.

> Example: John, a California resident, has cryptocurrencies currently worth $5.0 million and a cost basis in those currencies of $500,000, a potential gain of $4.5 million. If he transfers his cryptocurrencies to a C corporation in exchange for stock under the tax-free provisions of IRC Section 351, the corporation now owns the cryptocurrencies. A later sale by the corporation will cause a federal tax of $945,000. If the Corporation is formed in California, the state will levy an additional 8.84% tax of $397,800 for a combined tax of $1,342,800. John's individual combined federal and state tax rate could reach 52.1% or $2,344,500, more than $1.0 million in taxes!

This is a simple yet effective tax planning technique for long-term to minimize the tax bite on sales of cryptocurrencies. It also provides asset protection since it separates the tax liability from the individual, in case of disaster – huge gains one year, but even larger losses in a subsequent year – because the C corporation is a separate taxpaying entity. In conclusion, using a C corporation reduces the federal tax rate to 21% and isolates the potential tax trap of losses that cannot offset gains in a prior year, thereby sparing the individual taxpayer from potential economic ruin should the investment crash.

C. Avoid State Income Tax

C corporations, as standalone taxable entities, are taxed in the state where they are organized or do business. If John forms a C corporation in Wyoming (currently the favorite non-state tax for corporations), there will be no state taxes owed when the corporation sells cryptocurrencies; only the federal tax of $945,000 is owed, a savings of $397,800 in California taxes. In our example, the corporation will be formed in a state that has no corporate income taxes. Of course, care must be taken to make sure the entity resides and is taxed in a non-tax state, as California (and undoubtedly other tax-heavy states) may closely scrutinize such transactions.

Because distributions of dividends to John will be taxed both federally and by California, as long as he is resident there, avoiding dividend distributions makes sense. If access to the corporate funds is needed, John may borrow corporate funds[3] or receive a reasonable salary, which is deductible to the corporation, although taxable to John as compensation (ordinary income). If John is so inclined, he can wait until he is no longer a California resident, establishing residency in a non-tax state such as Nevada, Washington, Texas or Florida, or overseas, and then receive corporate dividends. By doing this, John avoids state taxes on the distribution, although he will owe federal taxes on the dividends (currently taxed at

3 There are dozens of cases in which IRS successfully reclassified a purported corporate loan to a shareholder as a taxable dividend. The loan must be real and IRS expects payments of interest and principal by the shareholder, and a true debtor-creditor relationship.

capital gains rates). Note: The state adversely affected by this planning may closely scrutinize the transaction and the economic substance doctrines will apply.

D. Gifts to Charity

If John makes large donations of cryptocurrencies to charity, the resulting charitable deduction will reduce his taxable income. The value of the cryptocurrencies held for 12 months or longer (long-term capital gains) is fair market value, not John's cost basis, so gifting highly appreciated cryptocurrencies held 12 months or longer will maximize John's charitable deduction. In this regard, sophisticated tax planning using charitable trusts may achieve large income tax saving and should be considered if the potential tax liability is significant. Basically, charitable trusts shift the potential gain from the taxpayer to a charity that will not be taxed, the taxpayer receives a charitable deduction and an economic benefit from the trust, usually income for the rest of the taxpayer's life. **Note:** If properly structured, these transactions should not invoke the economic substance doctrine.

E. Estate Tax Planning

For estate tax planning, there are grantor retained trusts, defective grantor trusts, dynasty trusts and family limited partnerships or LLCs, all designed to minimize estate taxes; but with the current unified estate and gift tax exemption at $11.4 million ($22.8 million for married couples), this tax planning is no longer a major consideration except for very large estates; consequently, thisTax Brief's focus is on income taxes, not estate tax planning.[4]

F. Retirement Plans

Retirement plans, IRAs, Roth IRAs, other retirement plans in which a taxpayer is permitted to invest in cryptocurrencies, do not report gains or losses, which makes them an excellent long-term investment vehicle. The catch is having enough retirement funds to make this an effective approach.

1. Roth IRA

If a taxpayer is fortunate enough to have a Roth IRA, not only is there no taxable gains or losses, income distributed from a Roth IRA is tax-free to the recipient! Of course, there are several requirements and restrictions, namely, one cannot receive tax-free distributions unless it has been in existence for at least five years and the recipient is at least age 59 1/2. A Roth IRA is a tax-free money machine. In fact, it is such an amazing golden goose that it might be difficult psychologically to actually take distri-

4 Estate tax planning can be an enormously complicated and sophisticated subject, but taxpayers should be aware there are estate tax planning opportunities for their cryptocurrency investments if the size of their estate warrants it.

butions from it because of its limitless growth potential. Unlike a traditional IRA or other retirement plans, there is no minimum distribution requirement.

2. Back-Door Roth IRA

For the dedicated long-term cryptocurrency investor, a Roth IRA is about as good as it gets for zeroing out taxes. If you do not qualify for a Roth IRA, but have funds in a traditional IRA or a 401-K plan that can be rolled over to an IRA, there is a method called a "back-door" Roth IRA in which funds are transferred to a traditional IRA and then rolled over into a Roth IRA. The rollover is a taxable event, so ideally, you'd want to do it when your taxable income is low, but once the funds are in the Roth IRA, all future income earned by the Roth as well as distributions to you are non-taxable.

Note: There could be a future limitation on the backdoor Roth IRA, but to date, this planning is mainstream and should not raise economic substance issues.

G. Tax Planning with Foreign Taxpayers

1. Gift of Cryptocurrencies

If you have foreign relatives or colleagues whom you completely trust, amazing tax planning can be achieved. Assuming in our first example, John has a potential $4.5

CRYPTOCURRENCY INCOME TAX PLANNING

million gain and a parent who lives in a country that does not tax capital gains. He can gift cryptocurrencies to a foreign relative who then sells them without paying U.S. income tax.[5] With extremely careful planning and no pre-existing arrangement or understanding, the foreign owner may later decide to gift proceeds to John and neither the owner nor John is taxed on the transaction.[6] Of course, it is safer for the foreign owner to retain and reinvest the proceeds offshore, or in a carefully drafted grantor trust (discussed below), rather than transfer the proceeds to John, as any subsequent income or gains will be taxed to him and the funds will become part of his estate for estate-tax purposes. Also, there is a solid asset protection if John does not own the assets and he is sued or runs into tax or financial trouble.

John's gift to a foreigner is taxable, but under the 2017 tax law, his unified estate and gift tax exemption is $11.4 million, so even if the gift is valued at $5.0 million, he retains $7.2 million of his exemption (Note: the exemption

---

5 Although foreigners holding certain U.S. source assets could have severely adverse estate tax issues, unless the asset is held in a foreign entity, cryptocurrencies (tangible personal property) should not considered U.S. source assets for estate-tax purposes (see Reg. §20.2104-1(a)(4)), thus foreigners hold them on a U.S exchange – this also means that John may have a power of attorney to direct the investments without an FBAR filing requirement since this is not a foreign account.

6 Receipt of a foreign tax is tax-free, but there is a Form 3520 reporting requirement if the total amount of gifts from foreign individuals totals $100,000 or more during a calendar year.

increases each year by the cost of living, currently about $200,000 per year).[7]

Note: Expect IRS to scrutinize this transaction if John receives the sales proceeds since there could be a circular flow of money from John to his parents and back to John for the purpose of eliminating taxes. Great care and planning are needed to imbue the transaction with sufficient economic substance. The safest route is to have the parent distribute the proceeds upon death through a will or trust, or make distributions years after the initial sale of the cryptocurrencies. In any event, the risks of engaging in this planning should be contrasted with the conservative alternative of selling the cryptocurrencies through a C corporation (taxed at the relatively low federal rate of 21%).

2. A Foreign Grantor Trust

Using a foreign grantor trust, rather than an outright gift to the foreign relative or colleague is a more complex but ultimately a superior method to achieving the same result; no tax on the sale of the cryptocurrencies, no tax on any subsequent income earned by the trust and estate planning for your family. Basically, a foreign grantor (rel-

7 Tax purists will note that John has an annual exclusion of $15,000 so add that amount to his remaining $7.2 million exclusion. The annual exclusion is also indexed for inflation.

ative or colleague, preferably of a younger age), forms a trust in a tax-haven (a country that does impose income or estate taxes), naming you and your family as the beneficiaries. During the life of the grantor, any income or gains in the trust and any distributions to you or your family members is tax-free.[8] The grantor must retain the right to revoke the trust and vest the trust's assets in the grantor's name for this concept to work; this arrangement eliminates U.S. taxes while the grantor is alive. Thereafter, the trust becomes irrevocable and U.S. beneficiaries of an irrevocable foreign trust have stringent reporting requirements (Form 3520-A) and could suffer adverse tax consequences. Often, the foreign irrevocable trust becomes a U.S. trust upon the grantor's death to avoid tax complications and onerous reporting requirements (with stiff penalties for non-compliance).

Funding the trust when the cryptocurrency has greatly appreciated is risky and must pass muster under the economic substance doctrine; using a foreign grantor trust to acquire cryptocurrencies before they appreciate in value is a much better approach.

---

8 Distributions are considered foreign gifts from the grantor so if the total amount of foreign gifts or inheritances from foreign individuals during a calendar year is $100,000 or more, the U.S. recipient has a Form 3520 reporting requirement.

If foreign parents want to give U.S. children funds for investment (including cryptocurrencies), the foreign grantor trust should be considered as both an asset protection vehicle, as well as a tax-free money machine (subject to Form 3520 reporting obligations) while parents are alive,

Note: In this context, a gift of cryptocurrencies from you to the grantor who then sells them and uses the cash to fund a foreign grantor trust runs the same risks discussed in paragraph G 1, so careful planning is required. Waiting an appreciable time after making the gift before the grantor sells the cryptocurrencies, then funding the trust over a period of time, or forming the grantor trust first then engaging in the gift transaction may give it the requisite economic substance to pass IRS or court scrutiny. In short, great care and planning are needed to infuse the transaction with sufficient economic substance.

H. Investing in a Qualified Opportunity Zone

If you want to sell your cryptocurrencies for a large gain but do not want to pay taxes immediately on the sale, there is a new tax-planning technique involving investments in Qualified Opportunity Zones (QOZ). Basically, gains from the sale of property are invested in a QOZ project within 180 days of sale. Taxpayers need to hold their investment for the long term. Taxes on the gains are deferred until year seven at which time, the taxpayer is taxed on 85% of the gain. If the investment is held for 10 years or longer, then profits from the QOZ investment is totally tax free! (See the article by Alan Seher attached hereto as Exhibit "D"). For example, Joe sells his cryptocurrencies for a $5.5 million profit and invests $5.0 million in a QOZ protect. He pays taxes on the $500,000 of gain that was not invested in the QOZ project. After seven years, Joe is taxed on 85% of his gain ($4,250,000) and using a combined federal and state tax of 30%, Joe's tax is $1,275,000. Assume his investment grows to $15 million after 10 years. If Joe sells his investment at that time, he pays no additional taxes. In effect, Joe receives $13,725,000 tax-free: $15,000,000 (initial investment of $5 M, plus gain of $10 M) minus taxes paid in year seven of $1,275,000.

Note: The QOZ rules presents a challenge, but if property executed, there should not be an economic substance issue since Congress has expressly authorized this result in the 2017 tax law. Nevertheless, complicated related party rules and other issues could arise in the implementation of this strategy.

V. Conclusion

Cryptocurrencies are causing angst for tax authorities as they grapple with how to tax them. Currently, IRS treats them as property so every transaction has gain or loss. This causes accounting and recordkeeping headaches for the investor. Of course, taxpayers who naively trade cryptocurrencies and do not report the gains, or do not keep records, are flirting with potential disaster. The goal of this Tax Brief is to prevent such an occurrence and provide tax planning from a C corporation to a sophisticated foreign grantor trust, with retirement plans, charitable contributions and gifting of assets as additional considerations.

Invariably, the informed taxpayer can dodge the lurking tax traps and greatly minimize or eliminate taxes through creative and proper planning. In closing, I want to wish you success and great wealth with this exciting new investment medium. As I tell my clients, your job is to make the money, mine is to make sure you keep it and I hope you found this Tax Guide beneficial in that regard.

Exhibit "A"

Federal Long-Term Capital Gains and Dividend Rates

TAX RATES SINGLE FILER	FROM	TO
0%	$0	$38,600
15%	$38,601	$425,800
20%	$425,801	--------
JOINT FILERS		
0%	$0	$77,200
15%	$77,201	$479,000
20%	$479,001	---------

Note: The Affordable Care Tax of 3.8% on investment income kicks in at taxable income of $200,000 for single filers and $250,000 for joint filers. Thus, part of the 15% tax rate and all of the 20% tax rates will include an additional 3.8% tax rate, thus raising the federal tax amounts to 18.8% and 23.8% respectively.

Note: There may be additional state income taxes on gains. Most states tax capital gains as ordinary income and not at a lesser rate.

Exhibit "B"

Notice 2014-21 - UPDATED October 9, 2019

This notice describes how existing general tax principles apply to transactions using virtual currency.The notice provides this guidance in the form of answers to frequently asked questions.

SECTION 2. BACKGROUND

The Internal Revenue Service (IRS) is aware that "virtual currency" may be used to pay for goods or services, or held for investment. Virtual currency is a digital representation of value that functions as a medium of exchange, a unit of account, and/or a store of value. In some environments, it operates like "real" currency -- i.e., the coin and paper money of the United States or of any other country that is designated as legal tender, circulates, and is customarily used and accepted as a medium of exchange in the country of issuance -- but it does not have legal tender status in any jurisdiction.

Virtual currency that has an equivalent value in real currency, or that acts as a substitute for real currency, is referred to as "convertible" virtual currency. Bitcoin is one example of a convertible virtual currency. Bitcoin can be digitally traded between users and can be purchased for, or exchanged into, U.S. dollars, Euros, and other real or virtual currencies. For a more comprehensive description of convertible virtual currencies to date, see Financial Crimes Enforcement Network (FinCEN) *Guidance on the Application of FinCEN's Regulations to Persons Administering, Exchanging, or Using Virtual Currencies* (FIN-2013-G001, March 18, 2013).

SECTION 3. SCOPE

In general, the sale or exchange of convertible virtual currency, or the use of convertible virtual currency to pay for goods or services in a real-world economy transaction, has tax consequences that may result in a tax liability. This notice addresses only the U.S. federal tax consequences of transactions in, or transactions that use, convertible virtual currency, and the term "virtual currency" as used in Section 4 refers only to convertible virtual currency. No inference should be drawn with respect to virtual currencies not described in this notice.

The Treasury Department and the IRS recognize that there may be other questions regarding the tax consequences of virtual currency not addressed in this notice that warrant consideration. Therefore, the Treasury Department and the IRS request comments from the public regarding other types or aspects of virtual currency transactions that should be addressed in future guidance.

Exhibit "B"

Comments should be addressed to:

Internal Revenue Service
Attn: CC:PA:LPD:PR (Notice 2014-21)
Room 5203
P.O. Box 7604
Ben Franklin Station
Washington, D.C. 20044

or hand delivered Monday through Friday between the hours of 8 A.M. and 4 P.M. to:

Courier's Desk
Internal Revenue Service
Attn: CC:PA:LPD:PR (Notice 2014-21)
1111 Constitution Avenue, N.W.
Washington, D.C. 20224

Alternatively, taxpayers may submit comments electronically via e-mail to the following address: Notice.Comments@irscounsel.treas.gov. Taxpayers should include "Notice 2014-21" in the subject line. All comments submitted by the public will be available for public inspection and copying in their entirety.

For purposes of the FAQs in this notice, the taxpayer's functional currency is assumed to be the U.S. dollar, the taxpayer is assumed to use the cash receipts and disbursements method of accounting and the taxpayer is assumed not to be under common control with any other party to a transaction.

SECTION 4. FREQUENTLY ASKED QUESTIONS

Q-1: How is virtual currency treated for federal tax purposes?

A-1: For federal tax purposes, virtual currency is treated as property. General tax principles applicable to property transactions apply to transactions using virtual currency.

Q-2: Is virtual currency treated as currency for purposes of determining whether a transaction results in foreign currency gain or loss under U.S. federal tax laws?

A-2: No. Under currently applicable law, virtual currency is not treated as currency that could generate foreign currency gain or loss for U.S. federal tax purposes.

Exhibit “B”

Q-3: Must a taxpayer who receives virtual currency as payment for goods or services include in computing gross income the fair market value of the virtual currency?

A-3: Yes. A taxpayer who receives virtual currency as payment for goods or services must, in computing gross income, include the fair market value of the virtual currency, measured in U.S. dollars, as of the date that the virtual currency was received. See Publication 525, *Taxable and Nontaxable Income*, for more information on miscellaneous income from exchanges involving property or services.

Q-4: What is the basis of virtual currency received as payment for goods or services in Q&A-3?

A-4: The basis of virtual currency that a taxpayer receives as payment for goods or services in Q&A-3 is the fair market value of the virtual currency in U.S. dollars as of the date of receipt. See Publication 551, *Basis of Assets*, for more information on the computation of basis when property is received for goods or services.

Q-5: How is the fair market value of virtual currency determined?

A-5: For U.S. tax purposes, transactions using virtual currency must be reported in U.S. dollars. Therefore, taxpayers will be required to determine the fair market value of virtual currency in U.S. dollars as of the date of payment or receipt. If a virtual currency is listed on an exchange and the exchange rate is established by market supply and demand, the fair market value of the virtual currency is determined by converting the virtual currency into U.S. dollars (or into another real currency which in turn can be converted into U.S. dollars) at the exchange rate, in a reasonable manner that is consistently applied.

Q-6: Does a taxpayer have gain or loss upon an exchange of virtual currency for other property?

A-6: Yes. If the fair market value of property received in exchange for virtual currency exceeds the taxpayer's adjusted basis of the virtual currency, the taxpayer has taxable gain. The taxpayer has a loss if the fair market value of the property received is less than the adjusted basis of the virtual currency. See Publication 544, *Sales and Other Dispositions of Assets*, for information about the tax treatment of sales and exchanges, such as whether a loss is deductible.

Q-7: What type of gain or loss does a taxpayer realize on the sale or exchange of virtual currency?

Exhibit "B"

A-7: The character of the gain or loss generally depends on whether the virtual currency is a capital asset in the hands of the taxpayer. A taxpayer generally realizes capital gain or loss on the sale or exchange of virtual currency that is a capital asset in the hands of the taxpayer. For example, stocks, bonds, and other investment property are generally capital assets. A taxpayer generally realizes ordinary gain or loss on the sale or exchange of virtual currency that is not a capital asset in the hands of the taxpayer. Inventory and other property held mainly for sale to customers in a trade or business are examples of property that is not a capital asset. See Publication 544 for more information about capital assets and the character of gain or loss.

Q-8: Does a taxpayer who "mines" virtual currency (for example, uses computer resources to validate Bitcoin transactions and maintain the public Bitcoin transaction ledger) realize gross income upon receipt of the virtual currency resulting from those activities?

A-8: Yes, when a taxpayer successfully "mines" virtual currency, the fair market value of the virtual currency as of the date of receipt is includible in gross income. See Publication 525, *Taxable and Nontaxable Income*, for more information on taxable income.

Q-9: Is an individual who "mines" virtual currency as a trade or business subject to self-employment tax on the income derived from those activities?

A-9: If a taxpayer's "mining" of virtual currency constitutes a trade or business, and the "mining" activity is not undertaken by the taxpayer as an employee, the net earnings from self-employment (generally, gross income derived from carrying on a trade or business less allowable deductions) resulting from those activities constitute self employment income and are subject to the self-employment tax. See Chapter 10 of Publication 334, *Tax Guide for Small Business*, for more information on selfemployment tax and Publication 535, *Business Expenses*, for more information on determining whether expenses are from a business activity carried on to make a profit.

Q-10: Does virtual currency received by an independent contractor for performing services constitute self-employment income?

A-10: Yes. Generally, self-employment income includes all gross income derived by an individual from any trade or business carried on by the individual as other than an employee. Consequently, the fair market value of virtual currency received for services performed as an independent contractor, measured in U.S. dollars as of the date of receipt, constitutes self-employment income and is subject to the self-employment tax. See FS-2007-18,

Exhibit "B"

April 2007, *Business or Hobby? Answer Has Implications for Deductions*, for information on determining whether an activity is a business or a hobby.

Q-11: Does virtual currency paid by an employer as remuneration for services constitute wages for employment tax purposes?

A-11: Yes. Generally, the medium in which remuneration for services is paid is immaterial to the determination of whether the remuneration constitutes wages for employment tax purposes. Consequently, the fair market value of virtual currency paid as wages is subject to federal income tax withholding, Federal Insurance Contributions Act (FICA) tax, and Federal Unemployment Tax Act (FUTA) tax and must be reported on Form W-2, *Wage and Tax Statement*. See Publication 15 (Circular E), *Employer's Tax Guide*, for information on the withholding, depositing, reporting, and paying of employment taxes.

Q-12: Is a payment made using virtual currency subject to information reporting?

A-12: A payment made using virtual currency is subject to information reporting to the same extent as any other payment made in property. For example, a person who in the course of a trade or business makes a payment of fixed and determinable income using virtual currency with a value of $600 or more to a U.S. non-exempt recipient in a taxable year is required to report the payment to the IRS and to the payee. Examples of payments of fixed and determinable income include rent, salaries, wages, premiums, annuities, and compensation.

Q-13: Is a person who in the course of a trade or business makes a payment using virtual currency worth $600 or more to an independent contractor for performing services required to file an information return with the IRS?

A-13: Generally, a person who in the course of a trade or business makes a payment of $600 or more in a taxable year to an independent contractor for the performance of services is required to report that payment to the IRS and to the payee on Form 1099- MISC, *Miscellaneous Income*. Payments of virtual currency required to be reported on Form 1099-MISC should be reported using the fair market value of the virtual currency in U.S. dollars as of the date of payment. The payment recipient may have income even if the recipient does not receive a Form 1099-MISC. See the Instructions to Form 1099-MISC and the General Instructions for Certain Information Returns for more information. For payments to non-U.S. persons, see Publication 515, *Withholding of Tax on Nonresident Aliens and Foreign Entities.*

Exhibit "B"

Q-14: Are payments made using virtual currency subject to backup withholding?

A-14: Payments made using virtual currency are subject to backup withholding to the same extent as other payments made in property. Therefore, payors making reportable payments using virtual currency must solicit a taxpayer identification number (TIN) from the payee. The payor must backup withhold from the payment if a TIN is not obtained prior to payment or if the payor receives notification from the IRS that backup withholding is required. See Publication 1281, *Backup Withholding for Missing and Incorrect Name/TINs*, for more information.

Q-15: Are there IRS information reporting requirements for a person who settles payments made in virtual currency on behalf of merchants that accept virtual currency from their customers?

A-15: Yes, if certain requirements are met. In general, a third party that contracts with a substantial number of unrelated merchants to settle payments between the merchants and their customers is a third party settlement organization (TPSO). A TPSO is required to report payments made to a merchant on a Form 1099-K, *Payment Card and Third Party Network Transactions*, if, for the calendar year, both (1) the number of transactions settled for the merchant exceeds 200, and (2) the gross amount of payments made to the merchant exceeds $20,000. When completing Boxes 1, 3, and 5a-1 on the Form 1099-K, transactions where the TPSO settles payments made with virtual currency are aggregated with transactions where the TPSO settles payments made with real currency to determine the total amounts to be reported in those boxes. When determining whether the transactions are reportable, the value of the virtual currency is the fair market value of the virtual currency in U.S. dollars on the date of payment.

See The Third Party Information Reporting Center, http://www.irs.gov/Tax-Professionals/Third-Party-Reporting-Information-Center, for more information on reporting transactions on Form 1099-K.

Q-16: Will taxpayers be subject to penalties for having treated a virtual currency transaction in a manner that is inconsistent with this notice prior to March 25, 2014?

A-16: Taxpayers may be subject to penalties for failure to comply with tax laws. For example, underpayments attributable to virtual currency transactions may be subject to penalties, such as accuracy-related penalties under section 6662. In addition, failure to timely or correctly report virtual currency transactions when required to do so may be subject to information reporting penalties under section 6721 and 6722. However, penalty relief may be avail-

Exhibit "B"

able to taxpayers and persons required to file an information return who are able to establish that the underpayment or failure to properly file information returns is due to reasonable cause.

SECTION 5. DRAFTING INFORMATION

The principal author of this notice is Keith A. Aqui of the Office of Associate Chief Counsel (Income Tax & Accounting). For further information about income tax issues addressed in this notice, please contact Mr. Aqui at (202) 317-4718; for further information about employment tax issues addressed in this notice, please contact Mr. Neil D. Shepherd at (202) 317- 4774; for further information about information reporting issues addressed in this notice, please contact Ms. Adrienne E. Griffin at (202) 317- 6845; and for further information regarding foreign currency issues addressed in this notice, please contact Mr. Raymond J. Stahl at (202) 317- 6938. These are not toll-free calls.

Exhibit "C"

26 CFR 1.61-1: Gross income.

(Also §§ 61, 451, 1011.)

Rev. Rul. 2019-24

ISSUES

(1) Does a taxpayer have gross income under § 61 of the Internal Revenue Code (Code) as a result of a hard fork of a cryptocurrency the taxpayer owns if the taxpayer does not receive units of a new cryptocurrency?

(2) Does a taxpayer have gross income under § 61 as a result of an airdrop of a new cryptocurrency following a hard fork if the taxpayer receives units of new cryptocurrency?

BACKGROUND

Virtual currency is a digital representation of value that functions as a medium of exchange, a unit of account, and a store of value other than a representation of the United States dollar or a foreign currency. Foreign currency is the coin and paper money of a country other than the United States that is designated as legal tender, circulates, and is customarily used and accepted as a medium of exchange in the country of issuance. See 31 C.F.R. § 1010.100(m).

Cryptocurrency is a type of virtual currency that utilizes cryptography to secure transactions that are digitally recorded on a distributed ledger, such as a blockchain. Units of cryptocurrency are generally referred to as coins or tokens. Distributed ledger technology uses independent digital systems to record, share, and synchronize transactions, the details of which are recorded in multiple places at the same time with no central data store or administration functionality.

A hard fork is unique to distributed ledger technology and occurs when a cryptocurrency on a distributed ledger undergoes a protocol change resulting in a permanent diversion from the legacy or existing distributed ledger. A hard fork may result in the creation of a new cryptocurrency on a new distributed ledger in addition to the legacy cryptocurrency on the legacy distributed ledger. Following a hard fork, transactions involving the new cryptocurrency are recorded on the new distributed ledger and transactions involving the legacy cryptocurrency continue to be recorded on the legacy distributed ledger.

Exhibit "C"

An airdrop is a means of distributing units of a cryptocurrency to the distributed ledger addresses of multiple taxpayers. A hard fork followed by an airdrop results in the distribution of units of the new cryptocurrency to addresses containing the legacy cryptocurrency. However, a hard fork is not always followed by an airdrop.

Cryptocurrency from an airdrop generally is received on the date and at the time it is recorded on the distributed ledger. However, a taxpayer may constructively receive cryptocurrency prior to the airdrop being recorded on the distributed ledger. A taxpayer does not have receipt of cryptocurrency when the airdrop is recorded on the distributed ledger if the taxpayer is not able to exercise dominion and control over the cryptocurrency. For example, a taxpayer does not have dominion and control if the address to which the cryptocurrency is airdropped is contained in a wallet managed through a cryptocurrency exchange and the cryptocurrency exchange does not support the newly-created cryptocurrency such that the airdropped cryptocurrency is not immediately credited to the taxpayer's account at the cryptocurrency exchange. If the taxpayer later acquires the ability to transfer, sell, exchange, or otherwise dispose of the cryptocurrency, the taxpayer is treated as receiving the cryptocurrency at that time.

FACTS

Situation 1: A holds 50 units of *Crypto M,* a cryptocurrency. On *Date 1,* the distributed ledger for *Crypto M* experiences a hard fork, resulting in the creation of *Crypto N. Crypto N* is not airdropped or otherwise transferred to an account owned or controlled by *A.*

Situation 2: *B* holds 50 units of *Crypto R,* a cryptocurrency. On *Date 2,* the distributed ledger for *Crypto R* experiences a hard fork, resulting in the creation of *Crypto S.* On that date, 25 units of *Crypto S* are airdropped to *B's* distributed ledger address and B has the ability to dispose of *Crypto S* immediately following the airdrop. *B* now holds 50 units of *Crypto R* and 25 units of *Crypto S.* The airdrop of *Crypto S* is recorded on the distributed ledger on *Date 2* at *Time 1* and, at that date and time, the fair market value of B's 25 units of Crypto S is $50. *B* receives the *Crypto S* solely because *B* owns *Crypto R* at the time of the hard fork. After the airdrop, transactions involving *Crypto S* are recorded on the new distributed ledger and transactions involving *Crypto R* continue to be recorded on the legacy distributed ledger.

LAW AND ANALYSIS

Section 61(a)(3) provides that, except as otherwise provided by law, gross income means all income from whatever source derived, including gains from dealings in property. Under § 61, all gains or undeniable accessions to

Exhibit "C"

wealth, clearly realized, over which a taxpayer has complete dominion, are included in gross income. See Commissioner v. Glenshaw Glass Co., 348 U.S. 426, 431 (1955). In general, income is ordinary unless it is gain from the sale or exchange of a capital asset or a special rule applies. See, e.g., §§ 1222, 1231, 1234A.

Section 1011 of the Code provides that a taxpayer's adjusted basis for determining the gain or loss from the sale or exchange of property is the cost or other basis determined under § 1012 of the Code, adjusted to the extent provided under § 1016 of the Code. When a taxpayer receives property that is not purchased, unless otherwise provided in the Code, the taxpayer's basis in the property received is determined by reference to the amount included in gross income, which is the fair market value of the property when the property is received. See generally §§ 61 and 1011; see also § 1.61-2(d)(2)(i).

Section 451 of the Code provides that a taxpayer using the cash method of accounting includes an amount in gross income in the taxable year it is actually or constructively received. See §§ 1.451-1 and 1.451-2. A taxpayer using an accrual method of accounting generally includes an amount in gross income no later than the taxable year in which all the events have occurred which fix the right to receive such amount. See § 451.

Situation 1: A did not receive units of the new cryptocurrency, *Crypto N*, from the hard fork; therefore, A does not have an accession to wealth and does not have gross income under § 61 as a result of the hard fork.

Situation 2: B received a new asset, *Crypto S*, in the airdrop following the hard fork; therefore, *B* has an accession to wealth and has ordinary income in the taxable year in which the *Crypto S* is received. See §§ 61 and 451. *B* has dominion and control of *Crypto S* at the time of the airdrop, when it is recorded on the distributed ledger, because *B* immediately has the ability to dispose of *Crypto S*. The amount included in gross income is $50, the fair market value of *B's* 25 units of *Crypto S* when the airdrop is recorded on the distributed ledger. *B's* basis in *Crypto S* is $50, the amount of income recognized. See §§ 61, 1011, and 1.61-2(d)(2)(i).

HOLDINGS

(1) A taxpayer does not have gross income under § 61 as a result of a hard fork of a cryptocurrency the taxpayer owns if the taxpayer does not receive units of a new cryptocurrency.

(2) A taxpayer has gross income, ordinary in character, under § 61 as a result of an airdrop of a new cryptocurrency following a hard fork if the taxpayer receives units of new cryptocurrency.

Exhibit "C"

DRAFTING INFORMATION

The principal author of this revenue ruling is Suzanne R. Sinno of the Office of Associate Chief Counsel (Income Tax & Accounting). For further information regarding the revenue ruling, contact Ms. Sinno at (202) 317-4718 (not a toll-free number).

Exhibit "D"

NIESAR & VESTAL LLP
ATTORNEYS AT LAW

90 NEW MONTGOMERY STREET 9TH FLOOR
SAN FRANCISCO, CALIFORNIA 94105
TELEPHONE (415) 882-5300
FACSIMILE (415) 882-5400
www.nvlawllp.com

To: Firm Clients and Contacts

From: Niesar & Vestal LLP

Date: June 21, 2018

Re: **Are You in the Zone for Opportunities?**

One of the new provisions in the December 2017 tax act was the creation of Qualified Opportunity Zones ("QOZ"). A QOZ is a population census tract that is a low-income community or a tract adjacent to a low-income tract that has been so designated by the Governor of a state. Each state has a minimum of 25 QOZs and a maximum of 25% of its low-income census tracts. QOZs have already been designated and can be found in an interactive map at https://nvlawllp.com/are-you-in-the-zone-for-opportunities/. There are over 3000 such zones. See, IRS Notice 2018-48.

QOZs allow an investor to invest gain, however derived, into a fund which owns a business or property in such a zone and to defer recognizing such gain until the earlier of the disposition of the QOZ investment or December 31, 2026. If the QOZ investment is held for 5 years, then 10% of the gain will become added basis to the original investment. If held an additional 2 years, another 5% of the gain will be added to the original basis. Finally, if the QOZ investment is held for 10 years, the basis in the QOZ investment is stepped-up to its then-fair market value. That means that you can sell stock, invest the gain in a QOZ business or real estate for 10 years and sell it in 2029, and only pay taxes on 85% of the original gain in 2026. The catch here is that the gain from the initial sale of assets must be recognized by December 31, 2026. But that does not belie the advantage of gain deferral and partial gain exclusion. Eliminating 15% of the original gain and assuming the time value of money at a 5% discount, there will be over a 40% tax savings, if held for 8 years.

Exhibit "D"

So how does this differ from Section 1031 exchanges? Currently, 1031 exchanges can only be used for real estate. With a QOZ, an investment may be made in a fund where 90% of the assets [both real and tangible personal property] are within the QOZ. As such, there is more flexibility with QOZs. Also, the source of the reinvested gain is not limited to real estate: it can come from the sale of a business; securities; or both tangible and intangible personal property.

Section 1031 exchanges require replacement property to be equal or greater in value to avoid gain recognition. With a QOZ, only the realized gain need be invested. As such, the investor may choose to recover his/her basis in the original investment for personal use or to invest in a different manner. [If more than the gain is invested, the non-gain portion is treated as a separate investment to which the usual rules apply].

Section 1031 exchanges require that replacement property be identified within 45 days and be acquired within 180 days of disposition or the original property. With QOZs there is no identification requirement, but there is the same 180 day requirement to reinvest.

Although a private or commercial golf course, country club, massage parlor, hot tub facility, suntan facility, racetrack or other facility used for gambling, or any store the principal business of which is the sale of alcoholic beverages for consumption off premises are excluded from qualifying as an eligible investment; there are plenty of other types of businesses and properties that will deliver this tax benefit.

The replacement assets must be new to the fund and acquired after 2017. They must also be new to the opportunity zone in the hands of the fund. That means that buying an existing business or real estate in a QOZ will not work. However, if substantial improvements are made to a property, that will qualify. Such improvements must be greater than the fund's basis in the property and be incurred within any 30 month period. That means that either new construction or a substantial rehabilitation of real estate will work to qualify.

Any investment must make economic sense. The QOZ helps tilt the decision tree to encourage investments in low income areas. California has not yet and may never adopt this new law, but the federal tax benefits are still available.

For an example, let's consider Thomas. Thomas worked as a project manager/software developer at AZ corp. He was well compensated and had amassed $500k in company stock with only a $10k basis. Thomas decided to start his own software company. If he sold his stock he would have $490k in gain, with about $100k in federal taxes owing as a result.

Exhibit “D”

Thomas decides to create an Opportunity Zone Fund for his new business. East Palo Alto has a designated Opportunity Zone that is reasonably close to both his home and where his potential workforce resides. Thomas attracts other investors into a new LLC, NEWCO., which is taxed as a partnership. NEWCO purchases a small building to house the operation for $500k and upgrades the building's HVAC, electric and plumbing and seismically retro-fits it as well, at a cost of $600k. NEWCO also buys new computers, software and furniture. To obtain his interest in the LLC, on September 1, 2018, Tomas sells his AZ stock and invests the $490k gain in NEWCO for a 51% interest.

As a result, Thomas does not recognize the income from the sale of stock. His $10k basis is returned to him to pay for his living expenses while NEWCO starts up.

NEWCO initially has a loss for the first two years and then Thomas' software takes off and NEWCO becomes profitable. Because Thomas only invested his gain into NEWCO, he has no basis in his LLC interest. As such, Thomas is unable to deduct his share of NEWCO's losses, but they are suspended until NEWCO begins to make money

On September 2, 2023, Thomas' investment in NEWCO passes five years. His basis in the sold stock automatically increases by 10% of his original gain, or $49k. On September 2, 2025, his basis increases another 5%, $24.5k. On December 31, 2026, even though Thomas still owns his interest in NEWCO, he is required to recognize his gain from the 2018 sale of stock. However, because of the increase in basis, only 85% of the gain is recognized, $416.5k. Thomas then owes $83.3k in federal taxes and must either use other resources or a loan to pay it. Thus, Thomas pays less tax and has deferred paying that tax for 8 years.

On September 2, 2028, Thomas' basis in NEWCO is stepped up to its then-fair market value. Thomas immediately sells NEWCO to AZ corp for $1B and pays no federal taxes on his share of the proceeds. Overall, a tax advantage to Thomas.

Should you have any questions, please contact Alan R. Seher, Niesar & Vestal LLP, aseher@nvlawllp.com.

NOTES

www.ingramcontent.com/pod-product-compliance
Lightning Source LLC
LaVergne TN
LVHW010546100826
845148LV00013B/2625
* 9 7 8 0 9 7 7 8 6 1 6 2 0 *